**Buy**  t

# Become a Successful Real Estate Investor by Owning Duplexes, Triplexes and Quads

By Alex Willen

© 2016 Alex Willen

All rights reserved. No portion of this book may be reproduced in any form without permission from the publisher, except as permitted by U.S. copyright law. For permissions contact:

Alexwillen+books@gmail.com

# Table of Contents

## Section 1: Finding, Evaluating and Buying a Property

Introduction

Finding a Real Estate Agent

Finding a Property

Evaluating the Property

Bidding and Closing

Getting a Mortgage

Insurance

Property Management

Protecting Your Property with an LLC


## Section 2: Advanced Techniques for Maximizing Rental Income

Introduction

Staging

Advertising

Section 8 Housing

Move Fast!

Allow Pets for Extra Income

**Fees and Utilities**

**Property Management**

**The Roof**

**Extra Tips**

**Conclusion**

# Section 1: Finding, Evaluating and Buying a Property

# Introduction

Hello there, and welcome to this book! My goal is to provide you with a simple, easy-to-read guide to all of the things that you should know before you go to buy a multi-unit property. Bear in mind that every real estate purchase is unique – each location has its own laws, regulations, trends and prices and every seller is a unique person with his or her own motivations. Because of that, there's no universal guide that will give you all the right answers, and that's why this is intended to be a high level guide. Chapters on your real estate agent and property manager are key, because these are the people you'll rely on to help translate this high level advice into action based on the specifics of your situation.

One thing that I feel is omitted from many of the real estate investment books out there now is information about the author. If you're looking to invest in Topeka, Kansas, you're better off taking advice from someone in middle America than a real estate agent in midtown Manhattan.

So with that, let me tell you a bit about me. I work in technology in San Francisco and decided to start investing in real estate in 2011. I began by reading books but eventually realized I'd need to get into the real world if I wanted to invest, so I found a real estate agent and started looking at properties. After a few, I realized that pretty much everything was out of my price range (real estate in the Bay Area is ludicrously expensive), so I recruited a couple of other investors with similar interest.

First, we agreed on goals – we wanted properties that would generate at least a little cash flow while our tenants paid off the mortgage. Property value appreciation would be nice, but given that we'd watched prices collapse during the last mortgage crisis, we didn't want to have to count on the price of the property for the return on our investment.

With that in mind, we started to look at the market. Single family homes were out quickly – there was no way the rent from one would cover our costs and mortgage payment, so we'd be sinking money into it every month. Since large apartment building were too expensive, that left us with multi-unit properties, up to fourplexes.

When we felt like we had a good handle on properties that would be good for us, we started bidding. Unfortunately, we did so far too timidly, given how hot the real estate market is here. We were constantly outbid by people offering all cash, and our first dozen bids were rejected outright. We knew we had to get aggressive, so we finally placed a bid significantly over the asking price of a triplex in Berkeley, CA sight unseen only a couple of hours after it came on the market. We knew we'd be protected by our contingencies (more on that later), and we ended up having our offer accepted. We closed the deal and took ownership about a month later.

Since then we've added another fourplex in Oakland, CA – both properties give us a bit of cash flow each month, and as an extra perk they've each risen in value.

I tell you this so that you understand my background and experience. If you're a new investor, just know that I've been where you are and have thus far had great success. I understand the challenges you'll face, and hopefully my experience will save you from encountering some of them.

## Strategy

There are plenty of viable real estate strategies that range from buying and living in your own home to investing in real estate investment trusts. Since I can't cover them all here (nor do I have the expertise to do so), this book will focus on the strategy I've employed – buying two to four unit properties and renting them out, with the goal of generating cash flow in the short term and holding them for the long term. Later in the book, I'll provide a framework for you to evaluate properties with this goal in mind.

## Finding a Real Estate Agent

If you're buying a property, there's almost never a circumstance under which you should work without a real estate agent. You'll find some advice out there telling you that the 2-3% your agent will take is a lot of money if you're purchasing an expensive property, but it's well worth it to have someone experienced on your side making sure you've done everything properly and helping you avoid pitfalls. I still use an agent myself.

### How to Find an Agent

There are a couple of ways to do this. First, ask around. Friends who have purchased property will likely have agents they can introduce you to. If no one comes to mind, you can always post on Facebook asking for referrals, or send a mass email at work.

Alternatively, the National Association of Exclusive Buyer Agents can be a valuable resource for searching licensed real estate agents. You can find their search form at http://naeba.org/find-buyer-agent.

### How to Vet Prospective Agents

Naturally, any agent you speak to will want to work with you, so it's up to you to ensure you find the right one. Don't feel compelled to work with one because they're nice or likeable – you're putting hundreds of thousands of dollars on the line, so you want someone who's both qualified and a good fit for you.

First, make sure they have experience buying multi-unit properties in your area – ideally your prospective agent will both be an investor himself and have purchase for others, though either of those should be sufficient. Ask them if this is the case, and if so ask for references and follow up with them. Second, ask some high-level questions about some of the information in this book – that should at least give you some basic confidence that your prospective agent knows what he's talking about. If your agent doesn't have any opinion on the use of LLCs or when property managers should be employed, for example, it's unlikely he's accustomed to dealing with this type of real estate.

Finally, make sure you're comfortable with your prospective agent's personality and style – this is someone you'll be communicating with frequently, particularly during the purchase process. My agent isn't pushy while we're looking for or bidding on a property – in fact, he's the first person to tell me to move on if a property isn't a good fit or if the price has been bid up too high – but if I'm not keeping up during the closing process, he'll be on me to ensure I'm delivering everything necessary from my end.

## Finding a Property

Once you've found your real estate agent and made sure that you're both on the same page about your investment strategy, it's time to start looking for properties. Early on, you should cast a wide net – even if something doesn't look like it's the kind of place you want to invest in, take a look anyway. There's as much to be learned from awful properties that you wouldn't touch with someone else's money as there is from those you'd like to invest in. In my early days, I looked at properties I couldn't afford, single family homes I had no interest in and a couple of places that needed to be torn down completely. I'll still go look at just about anything if I have time – you'll find that there's almost always something you can learn by visiting a property and talking to the seller's agent.

*Locating Properties*

Most properties go up on a multiple listing service – basically, this is like the classifieds for real estate, where agents list properties they have for sale. Your agent will have access to this and should be able to get you access as well. Ideally, he'll be able to set up automated searches for you that fit your parameters. Every time a listing for a multi-unit property under $625,000 in Alameda County, CA comes up, I immediately receive an email. This enables me to move very quickly on good properties right as they come on the market. You can find similar information on sites like Zillow and Redfin, but be aware that it's often out of date. Because of that, it's best to ensure you're getting info straight from the MLS. Don't let your real estate agent act as a middleman and send you properties that he thinks are a good fit - especially early on, you want as much exposure as possible.

There are other ways to find properties - canvassing the neighborhood, putting up signs, etc. When you take this approach, the goal is typically to find sellers with issues paying their mortgage or other problems before banks foreclose on them, so that you can get a good deal without having to buy the property from the bank. I don't recommend this for your first property, as it can complicate things and add risk. Some people feel the need to take this approach because it is hard to find a property that fits their criteria on the MLS at a reasonable price, but I live in one of the most difficult areas to find real estate and have managed to successfully purchase two properties. I recommend perseverance over attempts to find distressed properties.

## Setting Search Parameters

Your search will be unique, and no one knows exactly what you're looking for except for you (and hopefully your real estate agent). Because of that, you'll need to decide exactly what you want to look for.

### *Location*

I highly recommend buying somewhere that's local to you – it can be dangerous to purchase property outside of the area you're familiar with, even if it looks like there are bargains to be had. I wasn't especially familiar with the East Bay of California (where both of my properties are located) when I started buying, but my immediate area was out of my price range. As a result, I spent a significant amount of time visiting properties in person in my first year.

Your price range will give you a basic idea of where you can buy – this was how I settled on the East Bay – but once you've got that set it's important to understand the individual neighborhoods within a county or city. Oakland, CA is a great example of this – there are some really up-and-coming areas that are relatively underpriced, but I also found some properties that looked like extreme bargains until I realized that the neighborhoods were run-down and dangerous.

The property I ended up purchasing in Oakland is great because it's in a relatively poor area, but property is at the top of a hill and is across the street from a nice college. Because of the relatively low quality of the neighborhood, I got a bargain, even though the property is fairly isolated and safe. I never would have understood all of this had I not visited it myself – sometimes there's no substitute for driving to a property and walking around.

*Taxes*

One other location-based factor that's very important to familiarize yourself with is taxes and the related laws. In California, state property tax is 1% of your property's value, but cities can add fees that are either a percentage of the property or flat - in the case of both of my properties, these have pushed the overall property tax rate to about 1.4%. I thought that was high until I talked to a friend in Austin, Texas. They don't have income tax in Texas, but they make it up with property taxes, which are well over 2%.

Beyond the tax rate itself, one important thing to understand is when and how the value of your property is assessed for tax purposes. In California, the property is appraised any time it is transferred, which means that when you buy it, you'll set the value of the property at whatever you pay for it, and that's what you'll pay taxes on. The appraised value will not change after that unless you transfer the property (which is generally when you sell it). In Texas, on the other hand, the government can reappraise your property regularly, which means that if your property increases drastically in value, you'll find your tax bill going up rapidly as well. Your real estate agent should be able to tell you about the relevant tax rates and laws.

The last location-specific tax that may affect you is a business tax. Whether or not your rental real estate is considered a business that has to pay tax depends on where it is. I do not have to pay any business tax on my Berkeley property, but I do on my Oakland property. Make sure you research this before you buy - I found out the hard way by getting a notice from Oakland that I was delinquent on two years worth of business taxes.

*Price*

When you determine your price range, consider what you'll have to pay out of pocket, and err on the side of not stretching your finances too far. Assume you'll have to put down 25% of the purchase price for your mortgage down payment, and tack another 20% onto that number for repairs and closing costs (more if you intend to buy places that are clearly fixer-uppers). For a $500,000 property, this works out to $150,000. Ideally you won't have to spend this much, but it's better to have extra cushion – if you've got some money left over, you can always buy yourself a celebratory steak dinner after you close.

You should note that there are different rules and rates for loans beyond a certain size, based on what Fannie Mae and Freddie Mac (the government entities that back most mortgages) allow. In most places in the country, these limits won't be an issue, but if you're in an expensive place like the Bay Area, you can easily go over the limits with a multi-unit property and have to pay a higher rate. Your mortgage broker can tell you what the limits are when you're looking to buy.

When you set up your search parameters, I'd recommend putting a price higher than what you're actually willing to pay – you may find properties that are over your purchase price but can be negotiated down. That said, be sure you don't get attached to something that you can't afford and stretching your finances too thin.

*Property Type*

As mentioned, my strategy is to focus on two to four unit properties. Four is the cutoff, because at five units, mortgage brokers label buildings commercial residential real estate, and applying for a loan becomes a very different process (it's like buying a business as opposed to buying a property). As long as you keep it to four or less, you'll be getting a standard residential mortgage – the same type as if you were buying a single family home for yourself to live in.

That said, my preference is more units – with four units, as opposed to two, you'll get better economies of scale and will also be less exposed to cash flow problems if one of your units is temporarily vacant or a tenant stops paying their rent.

## Evaluating the property

Once you've identified a particular property, there are a few things you'll want to do to ensure you know what you're getting into if you buy it. These don't necessarily need to be done before you bid on the property, since you'll still have some time to withdraw your bid even after it's accepted, but you should make sure you do a proper evaluation before closing.

### Seller Disclosures

There are a number of standard real estate forms that should be provided by the seller with information about various aspects of the property, from who owns the appliances to whether a tenant has died on the property recently to whether anyone has operated a meth lab there (seriously). These are pretty straightforward, and if there are any items you can't understand your real estate agent can explain them.

The critical thing to understand about these documents, though, is that the seller is only required to tell you what he or she is aware of. That means you should certainly address anything negative the seller lists, but anything positive or absent you should evaluate for yourself.

In addition to the seller disclosure forms, you should get tenant estoppels – these are forms with basic information that the tenant certifies to be true. Make sure to check these to ensure that the tenant is on the same page as the owner about important details like the amount of rent and security deposit, as well as who pays which bills and who owns any appliances in the unit. Any discrepancies should be cleared up before you proceed.

## Evaluating Financials

While there are a few qualitative things you should be aware of (is the neighborhood extremely dangerous, are there particularly odd features to the construction that will be difficult to maintain), your evaluation of properties should mostly involve looking at prospective cash flow.

This is a relatively easy thing to calculate – the amount of rent you bring in minus all of your costs is your cash flow. Some of your costs are fixed, while others will require some estimation on your part. Subtract all the below costs from your projected rent, and the higher the number, the better the property.

*Fixed costs*

Mortgage payment – as long as you know the amount of your mortgage and the interest rate, this is easy to calculate, and there are lots of sites that will do it for you (here's one: http://www.bankrate.com/calculators/mortgages/mortgage-calculator.aspx).

Insurance – Talk to an insurance broker before you start searching to get a rough estimate of this. As a point of reference, for my properties, both of which had a price of just over $500,000, property insurance is roughly $1000 per year, and earthquake insurance is another $1000 per year.

Taxes – As discussed above, taxes vary at the state, county and city level. Make sure you're aware of all property and business taxes that will be levied on your property, and ensure you include those in your calculations.

Utilities – While evaluating a property, find out which utilities your tenants pay and which you will pay. For the latter, get a few months' worth of bills from the seller. Some bills, like garbage and sewage, will be fixed, while others, like electricity, will be variable. Usually the variable bills will be paid by the tenants, but if not, they should stay within a reasonable range. Electricity/gas may be seasonal if they are being used to heat or cool the home during extreme temperatures, but the yearly amount should still stay roughly the same from year to year.

Property management – This will be either a flat fee or a percentage of your rent. If you haven't gotten quotes from potential property managers, 10% of rent is a pretty safe assumption. Property managers typically also charge a fee each time they have to place a new tenant.

*Variable costs*

Maintenance – Ideally you'll only ever have to fix minor things, but the reality is that eventually, you'll have big repairs. Err on the side of caution here, as a couple of big repairs can wipe out your cash flow for the year. Newer properties should expect to have lower maintenance costs than lower ones. To reduce the variability of maintenance costs, you can purchase a home warranty that will cover certain repairs, but be sure to understand what's covered and what isn't.

Vacancy – When a tenant moves out, you'll be out some money. First of all, no one will be paying rent in the property while it's empty. Second, if you have a property manager, you'll likely have to pay their tenant placement fee. Third, you'll have to get the place cleaned up and presentable for new tenants – while damages can be taken out of the previous tenant's security deposit, it will not cover normal wear and tear, so things like cleaning house and touching up minor nicks and damage to the paint will come out of our pocket.

**Leases**

Understanding leases is a critical component of both purchasing and owning a property. When you purchase a property, the current leases come with it – for this reason, you should be sure to get copies of them before purchasing the property.

There are a few key components to look at when evaluating a lease:

*Duration*

Typically leases have a twelve month duration, and at the end of twelve months they convert to month-to-month, which means that they can be terminated with one month of notice from either the property owner or the renter. There are certainly exceptions – some properties offer month-to-month leases initially, and others will be willing to negotiate the length. Be aware that if you have a lease with unattractive terms, such as significantly below market rent, you will have to live with them for their full duration, so be sure to factor this into your valuation of the property. Rent control can also make a huge difference in how lease durations work - more on that below.

*Security deposit*

Tenants usually put down a security deposit that can be applied to any damage they cause to the property when they move out. The amount of the deposit can range widely – for a property owner, a larger deposit means more protection. Bear in mind that you can send tenants a bill for any damage beyond what is covered by their security deposit, but if they opt not to pay then you will have to sue them to recover your money, which, depending on the amount, may not be worth your time. Further, if your tenants have little or no money, they may be unable to pay regardless.

*Rent amount*

Perhaps the most critical component of a lease is its rent. As a prospective owner, it is important to understand how the current rents of your leases compare to market rates. The easiest way to find out is to look at rents for similar properties currently for rent in local listings on sites like Craigslist.

If rents are currently at market rate, then you can evaluate the projected cash flow of the property as it stands. If they are significantly lower, this may present an opportunity to buy the property for a relatively low price with the knowledge that you can raise rents when the current leases expire.

*Rent control*

One of the most critical things to understand about your property is whether or not the leases are governed by rent control. Your real estate agent should be able to help you determine this, and it should also be specified in your appraisal.

Rent control can be particularly troublesome for owners, as it greatly restricts your ability to make changes to the terms of leases. The specific rules of rent control vary by jurisdiction, but the policy of my properties in Alameda County, CA is relatively common – rent can only be raised on a yearly basis and the percentage increase must match the year's increase in the Consumer Price Index (CPI, typically from 1-2%). There are exceptions – for example, if you've made significant improvements to the property, you may be able to raise the rent accordingly. Be sure to familiarize yourself with rent control in the area – your real estate agent and property manager should be familiar.

Perhaps the most challenging part of rent control for an owner is that where it is in effect, you may not terminate a lease, even if it has ended. This is designed to protect tenants – otherwise they could be removed after a year unless they agreed to a rent increase, which would defeat the purpose of rent control – but it means that if your tenant is unwilling to leave, you may be unable to enact significant rent increases for many years. If you want to end a lease, you must find a legal exception to the rule, of which there are few, or negotiate with your tenant, which can mean paying them a significant amount.

*Other terms*

There are a number other, more minor provisions that can be included in leases. These include the allowance or prohibition of pets, smoking and even things like the presence of waterbeds. Usually these will be relatively inconsequential, provided that your tenant has a significant enough security deposit to cover any damage to the unit, but it is still worth reading the leases thoroughly to ensure that there are no terms that may cause problems in the future.

## Section 8 – Low Income Tenants

In some cities, there are programs that provide rent vouchers for low-income residents. The city assesses the ability of the tenant to pay for rent, and they pay the difference between what the tenant is able to pay and the actual rent directly to the property owner. These are commonly known as Section 8 vouchers.

There are advantages and disadvantages to Section 8 tenants, but my opinion is that for low-end properties, Section 8 tenants are highly desirable.

*Advantages*

The portion of rent coming directly from the city issuing the Section 8 voucher will be there reliably every month. In many cases, this comprises the vast majority of the rent. For example, one of my tenants in Berkeley, CA is living in a unit with a rent of $1400. She pays roughly $125 out of pocket every month, and the city covers the rest. Even if she is unable to pay, I will still get the vast majority of my rent.

Section 8 tenants are also well motivated to be responsible with your property – if they cause serious problems or you evict them, their Section 8 voucher can be revoked. In the case of a tenant who can only afford to pay $125 in Berkeley, a loss of her voucher basically means there is nowhere she can afford to live. Thus far, I have never had problems with my Section 8 tenants – the same cannot be said for those paying their full rent out of pocket.

One last potential advantage is that in some cases, Section 8 overrides local rent control. With my properties in Alameda, for example, I can levy rent increases beyond what's allowed by rent control provided the Section 8 board approves the increases. This is an important topic to discuss with your prospective property managers if you intend to rent to Section 8 tenants - mine have been phenomenal about getting rent increases approved.

*Disadvantages*

Section 8 tenants tend to have little or no income, so they can have difficulty paying their portion of the rent on time. While you may assess penalties for late payment, my advice is to be relatively lax, as long as you believe the tenant is making a good faith effort to pay you. Because this is a relatively low percent of the rent, as long as you're receiving it each month, even if it isn't on the first, I find it is best to be somewhat flexible.

The most significant disadvantage is that the Section 8 board will inspect your property regularly. I have repeatedly failed these inspections, despite the fact that my property managers are always on top of issues reported by my tenants. The most minor thing I've failed for was for peeling paint on the exterior of the house, which the tenant had not reported because it was inconsequential. The most serious was for a broken heater, which the tenant had not noticed because it was summer.

While you have a few weeks to fix minor issues like peeling paint, major issues like the heater must be fixed in 24 hours. Failure to fix issues in the allotted time can mean that the state's portion of the rent will not be paid until the issues are fixed. For this reason, I particularly recommend a property manager who is experienced with Section 8 if you are housing these tenants.

**Laundry Room**

Besides your tenants' leases, the one other lease your building may have is one for the laundry room. If there is a shared laundry room with machines in it, be sure you get this from the sellers.

Typically, this lease will have the owner take the change out of the machines and send a flat fee to the washing machine company or have the company get the change and send the owner a percentage or whatever is left after a flat fee. The bad news about these leases is the terms are typically very unfavorable to the property owner – they tend to last for 5-10 years and require a year or more of notice to cancel.

The good news is that your laundry room represents a miniscule portion of your income. In fact, it's really an amenity for your tenants – the money you receive may be less than what you pay for water and electricity to run the machines.

As long as you make sure that you have a copy of the lease and have a point of contact at the laundry machine company to ensure a smooth transition, you shouldn't worry too much about your laundry room's lease.

## Bidding and Closing

Once you've identified a property that fits your criteria, it's time to put down a bid! This can be a harrowing experience, particularly the first time, but if you're working with a real estate agent and understand the details of the bid, you can feel secure that you're not taking a huge risk by making an offer.

### Determining the Size of Your Bid

Depending on your particular market and the specific property you're bidding on, the amount you should bid relative to the list price can be vastly different. Take the example of a property listed at $500,000 - if you're in an area with very little real estate activity and the property has been on the market for three months, a bid of $400,000 or lower may well be reasonable. On the other hand, if you're in a very hot area you may need to bid $550,000 to have any hope of having your offer accepted.

So how you do know what to offer? Because every real estate purchase is unique, no book can tell you that. Instead, you'll be relying heavily on your real estate agent's expertise – this is why it's critical to have an agent that's familiar not only with your area, but also with the type of property you're trying to buy.

Bear in mind that the dollar amount is not the only component that the buyer will consider in your bid. All-cash offers make bids more attractive, since they mean there is no possibility of issues with a mortgage broker causing a loan not to go through. Similarly, the fewer contingencies (keep reading for more on that topic), the more attractive the bid. Even things like the timing of your bid can have an effect – the first time I had a bid accepted,

I put it in less than two hours after the property came on the market. This may sound like a terrible idea, but because I had contingencies in my bid, I knew I could lower or withdraw it later.

## Counter Offers

After your bid is submitted, the seller may decline, accept or counter it. Rarely will it be declined, unless there are a lot of bids and yours is much lower than the rest. While some bids may be accepted immediately, you should be prepared to receive a counter offer. If you offered $400,000 on the property above, the seller may come back with a counter of $450,000.

In a situation with multiple bids on the same property, the seller may opt to counter some or all of them. Typically, this counter will be above the highest offer, to give everyone a chance to move their offers up. You may also have multiple rounds of counter offers – if several prospective buyers move up, the seller may counter again to ensure that he is getting the highest possible bids.

The obvious question here is how you should respond to a counter. As with your first bid, this is incredibly situational, so you will be relying heavily upon your real estate agent. He should try to get as much information as possible from the seller's agent – how many bids are there, what the amounts of those bids are, whether are all cash, what contingencies they have and ideally their specific amounts.

Ultimately, when countered, you have three options – withdraw your offer entirely, leave it as is or modify it. In competitive situations, you will likely need to increase it to move up, but if you're dealing with a motivated seller and no other offers, standing pat may be the best strategy. This situation is really where a good agent will earn his keep.

Bear in mind that you can get creative with offers, since virtually all conditions of your offer are up to you. When dealing with a multiple counter on a competitive property, you might explain to the seller that you're interested in another property as well and must make a decision in a short timeframe, and thus your counter is your final offer and expires in 24 hours. It is, of course, still up to the seller whether or not to accept, so this kind of an offer typically needs to be high enough to make the seller unsure if anyone else will do better. Typically these sort of tactics aren't needed, but it's important to understand that bidding on a property is about more than just offering the highest price.

**Earnest Money Deposit**

If your offer is accepted, the first thing you'll need to do is put down an earnest money deposit (you can also celebrate, but bear in mind you've still got a long way to go before you own the property). This is typically 3% of the purchase price and must be sent to a title company via check or wire. The title company will hold it in escrow during the purchase process. If you pull out of escrow without a valid reason, the buyer gets to keep this money. Don't worry, though, as you still have several opportunities to pull out of the deal – these are the purchase contingencies written into your offer.

**Escrow**

With your bid accepted and an EMD put down, you're now in escrow. In general, escrow simply means that a third party holds the buyer's money until certain pre-set conditions have been met, at which point it is transferred to the seller.

The length of escrow is set in your offer, and is usually between 30 and 60 days. Sellers typically prefer short escrow periods, as everyone wants to get paid as quickly as possible. Your escrow does not automatically end after the specified period, but the buyer can choose to end it once that period is up. If you need one more day for a wire to go through, that usually won't be a problem, but if you're dragging your feet and the buyer feels you may not be able to close, they will likely end it and put the property back on the market.

**Contingencies**

Contingencies are your best friend when buying a property – they are clauses in the offer that enable you to back out with no consequences for a number of reasons. Each comes with a number of days for which it is valid, though contingencies do not automatically expire at the end of the specified period – you must sign an addendum to the contract agreeing to waive any contingency you have in place before it is removed.

Bear in mind that contingencies represent a chance of the deal not closing, so the fewer you have, the more attractive your offer will be to the seller. In some particularly hot real estate markets, your only hope of having an offer accepted will be to waive all contingencies, though this is certainly not recommended for your first purchase.

There are lots of types of contingencies, but some common ones that you'll likely want to include are:

*Inspection*

This gives you a specified number of days to have the house inspected. If you don't like what you see on the inspection report, you can back out. You will certainly want a property inspection (and one will likely be required by your mortgage broker), and I would recommend getting a pest inspection as well.

Beyond that, you may also want to get a roof inspection depending on the type and age of your roof. You can find some general lifespans for different types of roofs online – if yours is towards the end of its expected life, I recommend having it inspected.

After you get your property inspection, be sure to read it thoroughly, as it will highlight any problem issues that may require more specialized inspection.

*Finance*

The finance contingency gives you time to ensure that you will be able to secure a mortgage on the property before you commit to purchasing it. The mortgage broker will have requirements you must fulfill before the loan is granted, so you should ensure that your finance contingency lasts long enough to fulfill them.

Typically, these include an inspection as well as an appraisal. The inspection may require work to be completed before the close of escrow or a commitment to complete it in a certain time period after escrow closes. The appraisal has an independent appraiser look at market information, particularly the prices of other, comparable properties that have sold recently, to determine if the home is, in fact, worth what you have offered for it. If the appraisal comes in at a lower price than your offer, your mortgage broker may decline to give you a mortgage.

*Property Sale Contingency*

If you are planning to move out of a home that you own into a unit in the building you are purchasing, this enables you to withdraw from escrow if you're unable to find a buyer for your current residence. If you are in a competitive buying situation, it is unlikely the seller will accept this, as few others will have this contingency.

## Getting a Mortgage

Unless you're making an all cash purchase, you'll need a mortgage. The good news is that, provided your credit is good enough, there are plenty of institutions that will be happy to offer one. If this is your first mortgage, it's worth shopping around. Do this well before you have a property in mind – while you won't be able to lock in a rate, you will be able to find out who will give you the lowest relative rate, which in the case of a mortgage is the most critical piece of information, since fractions of a percent difference in interest rate can cost you tens of thousands of dollars over the life of the loan. Try a few different providers – big banks, credit unions and mortgage brokers.

## Points

Besides the interest rate, there is one other main number to your interest rates – points. A point is a fee that you pay up front to get a lower interest rate. One point is one percent of the loan value, so if you're buying a $500,000 property and putting up 25%, your loan value is $375,000 and a single point costs $3750.

Brokers will usually offer you between zero and three points, and depending on your strategy it almost always only makes sense to be at one of the two extremes. If you plan to sell the property quickly, it's unlikely that you'll recover the value of the points, so you shouldn't buy any. If you plan to hold the property for an extended period of time, you should purchase the maximum number of points available. The tipping point is usually between six and ten years, but since the ideas in this book are predicated on a buy and hold strategy, I recommend you get all the points you can.

## Fees

There will be some fees attached to the mortgage – usually something in the range of $800-$3000. Certainly get these in writing up front from your broker and ensure that you're charged the right amount, but don't worry about them much beyond that. You can compare between brokers and sometimes negotiate, but unless your mortgage is very small, you should opt for the lowest rate possible rather than deciding based on fees.

## Down Payment

Unless you're planning to live in the property yourself, you'll likely have to put down a 25% down payment (if you're living there, the number will probably be 20%). Ensure that you have this money readily available, as once you start the buying process, you won't have a lot of time to liquidate your holdings. Cash is best, and stock that's easy to sell is fine, but if you plan to use the latter, make sure you're prepared to pay the tax bill that comes with selling.

## Owner Occupy

One way to bring down your rate (and general cost) is to occupy one of the units you're purchasing. Depending on what the current laws are when you're reading this, you may also get tax benefits from doing this.

If you plan to owner occupy, be aware of the conditions attached to doing so – primarily, you must typically move in within a set number of days (your mortgage broker can provide the exact number). If you're buying a property with at least one vacant unit, this isn't a problem. If, however, it is fully occupied, you'll need to end one of your tenants' leases.

Make sure that at least one lease (for a unit that you would want to occupy) is month to month to ensure this is possible. Also, be sure you understand the impact of rent control – in rent controlled areas, even if your tenants are on month to month leases, you'll still find yourself unable to remove them. If all tenants still have multiple months remaining on their leases or are governed by rent control, you'll have to convince them to move out. If they're smart, this will typically cost you a pretty penny and greatly diminish the benefits of owner occupation.

## Insurance

When you spend hundreds of thousands of dollars on a property, you're going to want to insure it. On the off chance you don't want to, if you're getting a mortgage, your broker will insist upon it.

## Property Insurance

This is your basic insurance that covers the vast majority of damage and liability. It breaks down into several components.

*Rental Property Damage*

This is, as you would guess, coverage for damage to your rental property. You should have coverage for the full value of the structure, typically as determined by the appraiser at the time of purchase.

*Other Structures*

If you have a shed, garage or any other structure that is not part of the main rental property, this covers that.

*Personal Property*

This is typically less necessary for rental properties, since you likely not be storing your personal property on site. If you do store any of your belongings in storage areas on your rental properties, this will cover those.

*Fair Rental Value/Loss of Use*

If your property is so damaged that tenants cannot live in it, this will cover the lost rental income either until they are able to move back in and resume paying rent or until you hit your limit.

*Personal Liability*

If you are found liable for injuries of tenants or damage to their property, this covers you for their losses. Unlike all of the other coverage items, there is really no limit to how high your liability can go in the event of a lawsuit, so I recommend you opt for a large amount of personal liability coverage.

*Deductible*

As with any insurance coverage, you will have a deductible, which is the amount you have to pay out of pocket before the insurance kicks in. The higher the deductible, the lower the cost of your insurance will be, so determine

## Disaster-specific Coverage

In California, many property owners (myself included) opt to buy earthquake insurance. It comes at terrible terms – a deductible of 15% of the policy value and a price roughly equivalent to property insurance – but if the next big earthquake hits, regular property insurance won't cover any damage.

In other areas, you may want to look at property damage for common natural disasters, as virtually none of these are covered by property insurance. These may include hurricane, flood, sinkhole and any number of others. You know your geographical area best, so be sure to explore coverage for the type of disasters you might encounter.

## Umbrella Insurance

If you have a regular property insurance policy, but you're still concerned about your coverage (especially if the property is not held in an LLC), an umbrella insurance policy can add extra protection. It is basically additional liability coverage that protects you above the limits of your property insurance. An umbrella policy may also cover things that are typically not covered by property insurance - the umbrella policy will usually cover:

- Injuries
- Property damage
- Certain lawsuits
- Several types of personal liability (if someone trips over a crack in your property's concrete and is injured, for example)

## Property Management

One of the most daunting things about getting into real estate is the prospect of having to handle the issues that come with it. Particularly for those of us with full time jobs, the idea of getting a call at 4am when a tenant's toilet has sprung a leak and is flooding the house is not a good one.

Luckily, there are professionals who can handle all of this for you. There is, of course, a cost to this that you must weight against the value of the service. In making this decision, there are a number of things you should keep in mind.

### Factors to Consider

*Location*

If you're buying a property out of your state or even a few hours away, not having someone local to keep an eye on it can be a recipe for disaster. On the other hand, if you live next door or are owner occupying another unit in the same building, it may be more practical to manage it yourself.

*Experience*

Do you have experience managing a property? If you've been renting for your entire life and are accustomed to calling your landlord any time something goes wrong, you're probably not prepared to start managing your own property. On the other hand, if you've worked as a handyman it may not make sense to have a property manager outsourcing repair work that you could do yourself. Take an honest assessment of your skills and experience before you decide to manage a property yourself.

*Your lifestyle*

Consider how you spend your time, and whether you really want to dedicate a significant portion of it to managing your property. If you work full time and travel frequently, it's unlikely you'll be able to handle emergencies. Remember that there are people living in your units, and you owe it to them to solve their problems in an expedient manner – if you're in Europe ten times a year and leave them stranded with a broken water heater while you're on a transatlantic flight, you're going to have (rightfully) unhappy tenants.

*Fees*

The main thing that drives people to manage their own properties is the fact that you'll be paying a significant portion of each unit's income to a professional manager. There are usually a couple of components to these fees. First, expect to pay 7-12% of the rent from your property each month. If your rents are low, there may also be a flat minimum fee. My property manager charges 7% or a minimum of $110 per unit (I'm currently paying the latter). Bear in mind that many property managers manage single family homes, so because you have a multi-unit property (particularly if it has three or four units), you'll have some economy of scale and thus may be able to negotiate a lower rate.

The second component is a flat fee for placing tenants. Because it takes time to prepare a property and show it off to prospective new renters, you should expect to pay a flat fee of $500-1000 or percent of one month's rent. Because I want my property manager to be motivated to find good tenants, I insist that a clause is added to the agreement saying that if a tenant is evicted or leaves before their initial lease term is up that the placement fee will be waived for the next tenant in the unit. This should not be objectionable to a property manager, so I recommend you insist on it.

## How to Vet Prospective Property Managers

One of the challenging things about hiring a property manager is that you'll be placing a lot of trust in someone you don't know. As with your real estate agent, it is important to make sure that your property manager has the right experience to do a great job. Make sure that any prospective PM knows the area and is familiar with any particular regulations, particularly rent control. A few other things to take a look at include:

### *Experience*

Make sure that your property manager is used to dealing with your type of property and tenants. This is especially true if you have or intend to have Section 8 tenants - your PM absolutely must have experience with that program and the relevant Section 8 boards.

### *Service*

Get a very clear understanding of what you should expect from your PM. He should certainly handle day-to-day management of the properties and payment of the mortgage, but there are other activities beyond that to consider. Deal with the Section 8 board is certainly one if that applies. Taxes are another - in an ideal world, you can just introduce your PM to your accountant and have him send all your tax information directly, but he may just provide you with a year end summary to submit with your taxes. If you have business taxes to pay, find out whether your PM will pay those as well.

*Contractors*

Contractors are important, as they'll be the ones fixing your property, and you'll be paying them a pretty penny for it. Your property manager likely has contractors who he's used to working with, which can be a good thing and a bad thing. On the plus side, he should have a good relationship with his contractors and knows they are reliable and price things fairly. That said, since you don't know them directly, you're taking that on faith.

For that reason, you should get the names of all the contractors your property manager users and check on them. Ideally they'll have listings on sites like Yelp or Angie's list with good reviews, but if not you can still make sure that people like the general contractor, electrician and plumber are properly licensed. If you don't have a good frame of reference for the prices of repair work, make sure your contractor is okay with working with other contractors and have him get estimates from some others that you find on Yelp for your first few repairs. Ideally you should go with your PM's preferred contractors regardless, but this is a good way to ensure that they're not charging unfair rates.

*References*

Be sure to get references from prospective property managers. I don't recommend putting a lot of stock in these, since they're being supplied by the PM, but any good PM should be able to give you at least a couple of names of people who will speak highly about him.

*His Business*

Make sure you ask some basic questions to understand the basics of his business. Find out if you'll be working directly with him or someone on his staff, and if the latter, ensure that you meet that person. Determine how many units he's managing and how big his staff is – if it's a two person shop managing five hundred units, that should be a red flag.

*Software and Reporting*

You'll be counting on your property manager to keep good records, so you always have a good insight into what's happening in your property and whether you're making or losing money. Having everything well documented will also ensure that you're ready to go come tax time.

I recommend asking for a sample monthly report – make sure that it's something that you can read and understand. It should break down your costs (repairs, bills, property management, etc.) and your income from rent and your laundry machine. Also ensure that the property management software has a good way to save and categorize receipts from your repairs as well as bills.

## Protecting Your Property with an LLC

Disclaimer: I am not an attorney and none of this is legal advice, but it's a good starting point to have a chat with someone who is, in fact, a lawyer. One of the disadvantages to owning property is that it creates the potential for liability – if someone gets hurt on it, it's very possible you'll be sued. Your personal liability coverage will protect you from most lawsuits, but in the event of a very large legal judgement against you that exceeds your coverage, you'll be on the hook to pay the difference.

One way to protect yourself from this is to put your property in an LLC. Laws vary from state to state, so you should make sure you understand the ones relevant to you – Nolo provides great resources for this: http://www.nolo.com/legal-encyclopedia/limited-liability-company – but the general principle is that anything contained within the LLC is isolated from your personal holdings. Basically, if you get sued for an enormous sum of money far beyond your insurance coverage, the worst case is that you lose everything in the LLC – everything outside of it is protected. This is assuming you've formed and maintained the LLC correctly, and the best way to be sure of that is to consult with an attorney.

## Forming an LLC

There are a few ways to form an LLC:

### *Pay an attorney*

The upside to this is that your LLC will be formed by an experienced professional who understands the particulars of you and your property, so you can be sure that everything will be done properly. The downside is that you'll typically pay a relatively large amount (quotes I received from attorneys in California ranged from $1000-$1500) for something that isn't overly complicated to do. Given the relative simplicity, you should be able to negotiate this fee, but an attorney will always be the most expensive option.

*LegalZoom*

LegalZoom is an online service that handles many straightforward legal issues and transactions, among which is LLC formation (http://www.legalzoom.com/limited-liability-company/limited-liability-company-overview.html). It's much cheaper than an attorney (currently the price is listed at $149 plus your state fees), but through a series of questions on a web form, it's nonetheless able to provide documents that are relatively specific to your use case. In the common case of buying property and renting it out, this is typically sufficient.

*Do it yourself*

Finally, you can handle the LLC formation yourself. If you're not an attorney, I don't recommend it, so I won't expound on the possibility here.

## Transferring Your Property into an LLC

Unfortunately, mortgage brokers will typically not allow you to purchase property in the name of a pre-formed LLC – instead, you must purchase it in your own name then transfer it. Bear in mind that your mortgage will typically include a clause that allows the broker to force you to pay the remaining balance of the mortgage on a transfer of the property (as you would when you sell it), so be sure you inform them that you plan to make the transfer and ensure that they approve.

The actual move should be done with an attorney – this will, unfortunately, cost several hundred dollars, but it's money well spent to ensure that the property is placed into the LLC correctly, so that you receive all the relevant legal protection.

One other important thing to be aware of is that moving a property into an LLC counts as transfer of ownership, which in some states can be cause for the property to be reappraised and thus increase your property taxes. In California, there is a specific exception to the reappraisal rules if you transfer it into an LLC that has exactly the same ownership stakes as the property did pre-transfer (e.g. if the property is held 50/50 by you and another person, the LLC must be owned in exactly the same way - 50/50 with you and the same other person). Make sure you file the transfer paperwork correctly to take advantage of this exception and avoid a reappraisal.

**LLC Maintenance**

Laws vary from state to state, but typically there are a few things you must do to maintain your LLC's standing. First, in some states, LLCs have fees – for California, that's $800 a year. Second, you will likely have to file a Statement of Information, or something similar. This is a short form with some basic information about your LLC and its members that varies from state to state. In California, one must be filed on the formation of the LLC and every two years thereafter.

This topic is worth a short discussion with an attorney, as there may be other things you need to do to receive the legal protection of the LLC, like open a bank account for it and ensure that all rent is deposited there, rather than into your personal account.

## Whether to Form an LLC

Ultimately, whether you decide to form an LLC to hold your property is a question of cost versus benefit. The relatively high cost of a California LLC makes it less attractive, while in other states with lower fees it will almost certainly make sense. You'll have to understand your level of risk tolerance and decide accordingly

# Section 2: Advanced Techniques for Maximizing Rental Income

# Introduction

Now you know how to find, evaluate and purchase rental real estate. That's a great first step, but your end goal is, of course, to make as much money from that real estate as possible. Depending on the condition in which you take ownership of the property (empty vs. already rented) and local laws, especially those around rent control, you may or may not be able to make changes immediately.

If the property comes vacant, you shouldn't delay when it comes to finding tenants – while the property is unoccupied, you are still paying costs like property tax, insurance and mortgage payments. Thus it's in your best interest to get someone into the property paying rent, so that those costs aren't coming directly out of your pocket.

If it's occupied, make sure you do your research and preparation up front – once a tenant gives notice, you'll have limited time to figure out the best strategies for renting it out after they vacate. It's best to make sure you're well informed and prepared before that happens.

When it comes to renting out a property, there are a couple of things that you want to focus on that will allow you to maximize the money you make from your rental:

- Vacancy – An empty unit is a unit that's burning money, so one of the best ways to keep your money in your pocket is to be as efficient as possible in renting it out and ensure that it is vacant for as little time as possible. If your units are currently occupied, you should focus on keeping them that way – whenever they go vacant, that means cleaning and repair costs on top of the lack of rent coming in.

- Tenants – If at all possible, you want tenants that will remain in the property for many years (because that avoids vacancies) and will take care of your property. One thing that helps in finding great tenants is having as many applicants as possible, meaning you should focus on advertising your listing as broadly as possible (more on that later).

These are, of course, in addition to the fact that you want to charge as much rent as possible.

The advice in this section is designed to be clear, easy to implement and valuable. Not all of the tips here will necessarily apply to you, but that's okay – even a few good tweaks to the way your manage your rental real estate can mean tens of thousands of dollars in profit or more over the lifetime of the property.

# Staging

One of the best things you can do to help rent a unit quickly is to enable your prospective tenants to picture themselves living in it. If you've ever been house or apartment hunting, you've probably seen dozens and dozens of empty rooms with blank walls. There are some lucky folks with a great design sense who can immediately picture how they would furnish and decorate a home, but for those without that skill (yours truly included), it can be tough to look at an empty space and see a home that you'll be living in for years.

This is one of the reasons that staging has become popular of late, especially for higher-end rental units and homes. Staging is simply putting furniture and décor into the house before showing it, so prospective tenants see an inviting home instead of a completely blank slate. While it is traditionally associated with selling a home rather than renting, there are many situations, especially in competitive rental markets, in which staging can be well worth the cost.

One of the biggest advantages to staging is that you can use furnishings that highlight all the best features of the home and minimize anything odd or negative about it. Through things as simple as selecting the right color and size of furniture, you can control the feel of a home, whether that's making it seem spacious, dramatic or cozy.

Strategically placed furniture can also help to turn nonstandard features of a home from negatives that tenants don't understand into unique highlights of a property. If you have a house or apartment that is oddly shaped, something as simple as a table with some flowers in an unusual nook can make the home feel more personal instead of making people feel like there's a weird issue that they'll have to deal with if they live there. Remember that your prospective tenants are comparing your property to those that are standard, with large, rectangular rooms, so wherever yours deviates from that model, staging can help.

## Benefits of Staging

If staging is so great, you're probably wondering why everyone doesn't do it (and in fact, why it's actually rather rare among rental units). Well, nothing in life is free, staging included. Before you stage the property, you'll want to assess the cost of it relative to the financial returns you're getting from it. These can be tough to measure, but there are three basic benefits you should consider:

- Rent amount – A staged home looks and feels better than otherwise comparable properties, so when looking around the neighborhood at comps, you should consider how much of a benefit staging will provide and, accordingly, how much higher you can price your listing. Remember that even minimal increases in rent can be significant over the course of the year – if staging your property lets you bring in $50 extra a month in rent, that's $600 a year.
- Speed of rental – Because a staged house is more appealing, it makes you not only more likely to find a tenant, but also more likely to get multiple tenants interested. With more than one prospect, you are more likely to have someone who wants to move in as soon as possible, and even if not you have leverage to get prospective renters to agree to

start their lease earlier than they would otherwise to secure the property.
* Quality of tenants – The goal of staging is to make your property look and feel like a home, and if done properly it should help you to draw the kinds of tenants who will both stay in your property longer and also treat it better, since they feel it is their home and not a temporary space. Consider the types of tenants that would care about staging – young, professional families want to have a nice space to entertain or raise children, while college students who will likely move out after a year are unlikely to care about the interior design of a place. Staging will help you attract the former.

**Approaches to Staging and Their Costs**

There are a few routes you can take with staging:

*Do It Yourself*

This can be a convenient approach if you're about to start renting out the property in which you're currently living. In this case, all your furniture is already there, so by leaving it in the property you can both save yourself the cost of storing it temporarily and have a staged house with almost no work at all.

That said, it's critical to remember that the goal of staging is not to attract yourself, so you need to do an honest assessment of all of the furniture and decorations and decide what is going to be broadly appealing to prospective renters and what is too unique, quirky or downright weird. Certainly remove all personal items – pictures of grandma and grandpa are great for you, but other people don't want to see strange old folks in their new home.

Beyond that, understand if your furniture is suitable for staging. Traditional, simple items are best, as they will hold the broadest appeal. Your modern gray sofa and simple wood coffee table are probably great, but the beat-up lime green chair that you love because you've had it since college needs to get put into storage before any prospective renters set foot if your home. The more personal attachment you have to anything in your home, the more likely it is that it shouldn't be used as part of your staging material

One place where it may be okay to keep unique pieces and room setups is in extra rooms. People will have their own ideas about what a kitchen, bedroom and living room should look like, but staging can give them an idea for how they might use an extra room, especially one that's too small for a bedroom. A desk and chair turn it into a functional office, where some children's furniture (though without a floor littered with toys) can make it a playroom. In this way, you can make the extra space in a unit feel valuable instead of wasted.

Similarly, if you have rooms that have been set up for a specific purpose, it may be best to leave them set up that way. If you've sunk a lot of money into theater-style seating and a high-end projector for your theater room, you should leave it there and put a movie on while you show the property (though probably best to keep it family-friendly – showing *Saw* may drive away some possible tenants). Similarly, if you have a man cave, consider taking out some of the neon light-up beer signs, but leave the pool table – that can help give the room some character.

*Hire a Professional*

If you just had a tenant move out, your unit is probably empty, so unless you have a storage unit full of furniture somewhere, it probably doesn't make sense for you to stage it yourself. Naturally, there are people who do keep storage units full of furniture for this very purpose and will happily stage your home – for a price.

With professionals, in addition to the actual furniture, you're getting the benefit of their expertise. They have done this hundreds of times and thus have had the benefit of seeing hundreds of homes and their layouts. They understand what the current trends in décor are, and they will be able to stage your property such that is it appealing to the widest possible group of people.

Prices can range broadly depending on your home size and city. Obviously, the bigger your property is, the more staging it will require, and thus the more expensive it will be. Prices can run anywhere from $1000-$6000, but staging professionals will generally walk through your property and give you a free estimate to determine the exact price.

*Virtual Staging*

More recently, a concept called virtual staging has arisen. As the name implies, there is no actual physical furniture involved. Instead, you submit images of your property to a service online, and they digitally insert furniture and décor for your listing images. While this does not have the same effect as actually staging the home, it can help to draw in more prospective renters by giving them a better first impression. It is also much cheaper, usually a few hundred dollars (with prices increasing based on the number of photos you would like staged).

If you do decide to stage your home virtually, make sure that the company doing it follows the same principles as regular staging; keep the furniture simple and in neutral colors, so that it appeals to the widest possible audience. This will not only be good for renting your unit out today, but it will also allow you to save all of your images and reuse them time and time again when the property goes back on the rental market.

## Should I Stage?

The main question to ask is whether the price of staging will outweigh the benefit. Consider the price as compared to the benefits listed above. Also consider outside factors – if you are in an incredibly hot rental market in which properties are rented the day the go on the market, staging may not be worth your time. If there is lots of competition, however, staging can be immensely valuable in helping to make your unit stand out and ensure that it does not stay vacant for long. If $2000 of staging allows you to get a renter one month faster and the rent is $3000, it's a no-brainer.

# Advertising

No one will rent your property if they don't know it exists. In most markets, there is a dominant rental platform (in the Bay Area and plenty of other cities, it's Craigslist), so it's tempting to just list your unit on there and call it a day. That will often do the job, but with a little bit of extra effort, you can advertise even more broadly, and more advertising means more eyes on your property, which means more prospective renters.

Beyond that, the quality of your listing is important – spending an hour ensuring that it is perfect and highlights all the great qualities of your property is an excellent use of time.

**Where to Advertise**

Naturally, the first place you should advertise these days is online – that's where most people will be looking for your listing, so it's where you should spend most of your time.

*Craigslist*

Craigslist has endured for many years as the primary place to find rental units in most of America, despite the fact that it has a rather outdated design. To advertise on Craigslist, go to craigslist.org and find your city. On the left side of the screen click on "post to classifieds," pick "housing offered" and click continue. Choose "apts/housing for rent" then pick your particular neighborhood. Once you've done that, you'll see the main listing page, where you add all of your information and submit your listing. Ensure that you provide enough detail and great images – more on how to craft a great listing below.

*Zillow / Redfin / Trulia*

These three sites are primarily known for their real estate listings, but they also offer the option to list your property for rent. Often large apartment buildings will list their units here, which means that prospective apartment hunters will often browse these listings, so if you have a one to three bedroom apartment or an equivalently sized house that might appeal to these renters, these are great places to list it. All of the listing information is roughly the same as what Craigslist requires, so you can just copy and paste from your CL listing – that means listing on these sites takes just a matter of minutes.

*Other Internet Listing Sites*

There are dozens of these, but a few worth mentioning are RadPad, Oodle and HotPads. While there is nothing exceptional about any of these, the incremental time you can spend posting the same information to these sites you already did to Craigslist may be worth it.

*Social Networks*

If you have a significant following on sites like Twitter and Facebook, they are great places to promote your listings. You can simply link to your Craigslist post, so there is no need for any additional work, and you may attract better tenants by going through your own network. You can also offer referral bonuses here – encourage people that you know to share your posting, and if any of them successfully yield a tenant for you, reward them for it. Since you're advertising to your personal network, the reward need not be big – a $50 Starbucks gift card and the prospect of helping out a friend is usually more than enough to get people to click the share button.

*Local Newspapers*

Local newspapers often get twice the bang for your buck, since many have online rental listings in addition to those in the physical papers. These may have costs associated with posting, though they are typically low enough to be worth it.

*Student / Military / Veteran Housing*

If your rental property is near a university or a military base, you have a built in set of prospective renters. In these situations, there are frequently specific posting sites or discussion forums that cater to students or members of the military, so be sure to seek those out if they apply for you. In these cases, it may also be worth posting on physical bulletin boards in place like student and career centers.

Especially with students, it helps to know the specifics of their situation – most importantly, when they'll be renting. You'll see a large influx of students at the beginning of the school year, making this a very competitive time for renters and thus a great time to have your unit on the market. If you need to rent at another point in the year, though, remember that the beginning of every semester will see new students looking for housing, though fewer than at the beginning of the year.

## Creating a Great Listing

Putting your listing on a hundred sites is good, but quality is just as important as quantity (and thankfully it's easy to have both). With a little time, you can craft the kind of listing that will draw in anyone who looks at it.

*Pictures*

Pictures are incredibly important, and in this day and age there is no excuse for having bad ones or none at all. When you take them, ensure that your property is clean and well maintained. When taking pictures of the outside, make sure the gardener has just come, so that the lawn looks perfectly manicured and plants are well trimmed. You should also strive to take photos during good weather – people like to picture themselves in their new home on a sunny afternoon, not in the midst of a blizzard. Similarly, those inside should be taken immediately after a cleaner has come.

You should ensure you highlight the best features of your house in the photos, whether that is a big backyard, a beautiful kitchen with modern appliances or a recently remodeled bathroom. Take pictures at a time of day when there is plenty of light, and add lamps or use your flash as necessary. There is also no shame in a little Photoshop work to cover up small blemishes like stains on the carpet or chips in your paint. If you don't know how to use Photoshop, you can always hire someone for simple touch ups on a site like Fiverr.

Ensure you save your pictures – in the future you may want to list your unit after a tenant has given notice that they are going to move out but while they are still in the unit. When this happens, it is much better to have high quality pictures on hand instead of having to coordinate with your tenant and take photos with their furniture and personal items throughout the property.

*Details*

Saying that you have a two bedroom, one bathroom home isn't enough – you should highlight the good qualities of those, whether it's a lot of natural light, great views or a lot of space. Anything negative should be addressed euphemistically if at all – for example:

- A small house should be referred to as cozy
- A house near a loud freeway makes for an easy commute
- Locations away from shops and other conveniences are quiet and peaceful
- An apartment over a loud bar is in a central location near nightlife

Fill in as much information as possible in any specific fields provided by the listing site – things like square footage, rent, pets and number of beds and baths. It's fine to have that information in your description, but if there is a specific field for something, that typically means that users can search based on the values in those fields. That means that if a prospective tenant limits his search to apartments that allow dogs on Craigslist, but you have only written that you allow dogs in the description and not checked the "allows dogs" checkbox, that person will never see your listing.

## Examples

Here are a few examples – first, two excellent listings:

$4595 / 3br - 1700ft² - Pets OK! Beautiful Remodeled SFH walk to Google! (mountain view)

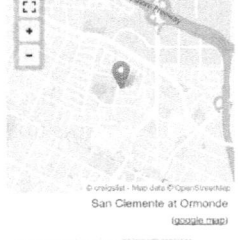

San Clemente at Ormonde
(google map)

3BR / 2Ba   1700ft²   available now

cats are OK - purrr
dogs are OK - wooof
house
w/d in unit
no smoking
attached garage

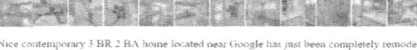

Nice contemporary 3 BR 2 BA home located near Google has just been completely remodeled, finished in October 2016.
Beautiful hardwood floors exist throughout most of the house and have just been redone
Large spacious open living room and family room combination!
Kitchen has been completely remodeled with new cabinets, white quartz counters, tile floors, and all stainless steel appliances
Separate dining area off of kitchen.
There is also a large add-on room off the living room
Bathrooms also have been completely remodeled - new shower/tub, vanities, counters, floors
2-car garage.
400 ft from large park and tennis courts!
Good Schools - Theuerkauf Elementary School K-5 (2 blocks away), Crittenden Middle School 6-8, Los Altos High School
1-2 minutes from 85/101 and Google.
Extremely Clean! Shows Great!
Very quiet neighborhood - almost no thru traffic (San Clemente Way is only 1 block long and so street has a private feel to it).
Available Now.

You may see a virtual tour of the property here:
http://tours.ewalk.com/public/vtour/display/620891?idx=1

Call show contact info for further information or to set up an appointment to view the property.

Here, you'll note that the listing has detail both in the title and in the structured information in the right sidebar (pets are allowed, the square footage is listed, and the washer/dryer and garage are both included for anyone who might include those in their search). The pictures are high quality and were taken when the house was in pristine condition. The listing also includes information on local schools and nearby amenities like a park and tennis courts.

# $3900 / 1br - 750ft² - Amazing Apartment with Office (noe valley)

image 1 of 18

1220A Sanchez Street
(google map)

1BR / 1Ba  750ft²  available nov 20

sunday 2016-11-20

dogs are OK - wooof
apartment
laundry in bldg
no parking

This is an amazing one bedroom apartment with office in the Heart of Noe Valley.

Just two blocks from 24th street restaurants, boutiques, and Weekend Farmers Market. Also, just one block from the J-Church MUNI line to downtown. You can easily hop on the freeway to drive to Silicon Valley. Google, Apple, and Genentech all have Buses that stop in the neighborhood.

The apartment is in a beautiful Edwardian building from 1915. Lovely details include:

- Hardwood Floors
- Sunny Bay Windows
- Claw foot tub
- Large eat-in kitchen
- Office off the landscaped garden filled with tropical plants and a fountain
- Spacious living room with wood paneling, crown moulding and the most amazing and rare feature - A Spinning Murphy Bed! Great for guests visiting from out of town.

Included is shared washer and dryer in the basement, storage, and 3 closets in the apartment.

Rent is $3,900. A deposit of $3,900 is required and will be refunded upon vacancy as long as the unit is left in good condition. Water and garbage is included. Tenant pays for the Electrical and Gas bill with PG&E.

There will only be one open house this Sunday, November 20th, from 1pm to 3pm.

This apartment is unfurnished and is now available for rent.

Please contact Mike to confirm you will be attending the open house this Sunday afternoon.

Thanks,

Mike O.

Again, excellent photos, detail around the property (including highlighting a differentiator in the title – most apartments of this size in San Francisco do not have offices, so adding that up front is a good idea) and information about when to view it.

Now, a couple of bad examples:

Pretty much everything about this is bad – poorly written, very little detail and no pictures at all. Even if your property isn't beautiful, if you don't have any images at all people will assume the absolute worst.

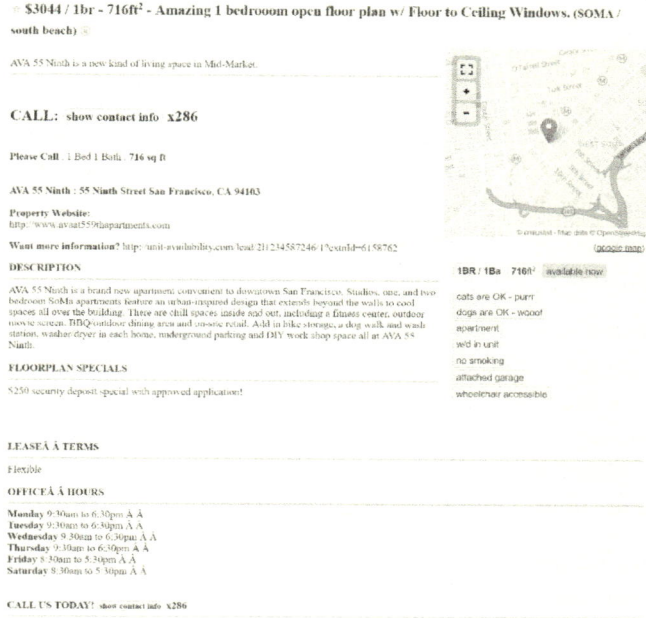

This ad is clearly designed to get you to go to the link listed under "Want more information?" Unfortunately, the lack of pictures mean that many people won't even look at the listing detail to find that link. It's fine to point to another listing on your own website if you have some, but you still need to have a good Craigslist posting, so people are at least interested enough to click on that link.

# Section 8 Housing

One of the best ways to get your property rented as quickly as possible is to ensure that your rental audience is as big as possible, and one excellent way to both expand your prospective set of renters and to get free, effective advertising is to open your unit up to Section 8 tenants.

Section 8 is a government program, generally operated at the city level, that provides housing vouchers to low income individuals and families. You do not have to discount your rent or restrict your audience to only Section 8 tenants – opening it up to those with vouchers simply expands your pool of prospective renters.

While Section 8 tenants are sometimes stigmatized because they are low income, I have had numerous Section 8 tenants and found them to be no better or worse than their non-Section 8 counterparts. They also have a few major advantages:

- City payment – The tenant pays his or her portion of the rent, which may be anywhere from 10-90% of the total, and the city pays the rest. Even if the tenant has problems and is temporarily or permanently unable to pay, you can count on getting the city's portion of the rent on time and in full every month.
- Tenant problems – While some people stereotype Section 8 tenants as poorly behaved because they are low income, they are actually better motivated than non-Section 8 tenants to communicate with you and pay their rent. This is because Section 8 vouchers are limited, typically with a long wait

list, and if a Section 8 tenant is evicted or has repeated problems, his voucher can be revoked. Someone who has a voucher covering 90% of his rent is very likely to become homeless if he loses it, which means that he's well motivated to keep it.
- Advertising – City Section 8 services generally have listings of properties that permit Section 8 tenants, and these are the primary places these tenants look for housing, making them incredibly effective and targeted. This is in addition to the fact that they are almost universally free, since providing this housing is a service to the city.

## Opening Your Property to Section 8

Because every city's program is independently operated, the process for allowing Section 8 tenants is not always the same. In general, though, the best thing to do is visit the website of your local Section 8 authority. These are usually named after the city – for example, in the Bay Area these programs are governed by The Oakland Housing Authority and the Berkeley Housing Authority. You should be able to find the correct government body by Googling "Section 8 <your city's name>."

If the instructions are not clear on the web site, it is worth calling in or visiting the local office – employees there will be happy to help, since it is always better for their program to have more units available to Section 8 tenants. You will generally just have to fill out some paperwork and register your property, though this may not be necessary unless you end up renting to a Section 8 tenant.

Once you've connected with the local office, ensure that in addition to listing your property on the Section 8 listings, you should also include the fact that you accept Section 8 tenants on listings you place on Craigslist and elsewhere, since tenants with Section 8 vouchers may be looking there.

Note that once you do have a Section 8 tenant in place, you will need to have an ongoing relationship with the governing housing authority. They will typically inspect the property at least once a year and require you to make any necessary repairs, and you will be required to submit any requests for rent increases to them as well.

### Rent Increases with Section 8

In some cities, there is one huge but underappreciated benefit of Section 8 – if your property is in an area in which rent adjustments are governed by rent control laws, Section 8 properties may be exempt from those laws. This is not to say that you can increase rents indiscriminately, but rather that you may make any adjustments to rent provided they are approved by the city housing board governing your local Section 8 program.

While this process is a bit more opaque than clearly written rent control laws, those laws are often so strict that anything is better. In the Bay Area of California, for example, most cities only permit rent increases of the same percentage of the previous year's CPI increase. The CPI (consumer price index) is a measure of how much inflation has caused overall prices of consumer goods to increase, and it is usually 2% or less, which means you generally won't be able to increase rents more than 2% per year.

I've had great success getting significantly larger increases than this for my Section 8 housing – while the local housing authorities did not have to approve these increases, it is in their interest to allow reasonable rent raises to incentive landlords to continue allowing Section 8 tenants in their units. The increased rents were still significantly below market rates, but far better than they would have been had they been governed by local rent control.

# Move Fast!

One of the best ways to make more money from your rental property is to make sure it doesn't sit vacant. Remember that every day it sits empty is a day that you're paying for insurance, your mortgage and all the other costs associated with property ownership without rent to cover them. Going a month or more without a tenant can put a huge dent in your profits for the year, so you should strive to have the property sit vacant for no more than two weeks at a time and ideally less than that.

As soon as you know that you plan to rent the property, you should start preparing. That may be when you're in escrow if you're buying a property with no tenants currently living there or when a current tenant gives notice that they are going to move out of a property you already own. Either way, it should rarely be a surprise that you're going to have to find tenants, so start your preparation as early as possible.

## Do Your Prep Work

There are a number of things you can get started on before you're actually ready to rent a unit out:

- Do your research – This is the time to look at rental listings sites and determine how many units similar to yours are on the market and what their listed rents are. It's a good idea to go to some open houses to see how many prospective renters show up. If they're packed, you can price your listing at or above comparable units, but if they're near empty you may want to undercut your competition to ensure your unit does not sit vacant while others are rented.

- Prepare your listings – Write everything up in a Word document, so that all you have to do is copy and paste to get your listing up immediately when you're ready. Get your photos together in advance as well.
- Assess needed repairs – Whether you have a tenant who is vacating a property or you are purchasing a new one, you should be able to get into the house to assess its condition. Take pictures so that you have a record of needed repairs.
- Schedule cleaning and repairs – If you know the date that the property will be empty, there is no need to wait until then to schedule the necessary work. Instead, line up repairmen, gardeners, appliance deliveries and cleaners to be at the property immediately after it goes vacant.

## Show the Unit Early and Get It Rented Fast

Most states have laws that require tenants to allow you to show the property during reasonable hours with reasonable notice. Take advantage of these, and show off the property to prospective tenants while it is still occupied. If you coordinate this with the repairs and cleaning properly, you can have a very brief vacancy period.

Another strategy for minimizing vacancy is to get multiple interested tenants. When you are selling a property, multiple offers give you leverage, and the same applies to renting. Let your prospects know that there are multiple people interested and that you would like your unit occupied as soon as possible – often they will be willing to move their lease start date up by a week or two even if they aren't going to move in at that point, just to ensure they secure the unit. Remember, though, that all tenants are not equal – if you have multiple prospects but some are clearly worse than others (due to poor credit history, lack of employment, previous evictions or similar factors), it's better to just take one of the good tenants, as a week of vacancy is much less expensive than a future eviction.

# Allow Pets for Extra Income

Many landlords don't consider pets at all, which is understandable given that four extra legs (not to mention claws and teeth) can put significant extra wear and tear on your unit. That said, allowing pets has two inherent advantages – you can charge more rent and you increase the size of your prospective rental pool.

**Pet Charges and Deposit**

People love their pets. As the owner of a big husky/shepherd mix, I can personally attest that there are few things I wouldn't do for my dog. When it comes to renting, I'm more than happy to throw in a few extra dollars each month on his behalf. The same is true of just about every other dog owner I know.

That said, much as I love my dog, it would be understandable if you didn't want him in your unit – he's 70 pounds and, frankly, a little nuts. That's okay, though – as an owner, allowing pets isn't just a yes or no question. It's up to you exactly which pets you want to allow, and my recommendation is to always allow cats, since they tend to be small and clean, as well as dogs under 25 pounds. If that sounds like too much, at the very least consider allowing dogs under 10 pounds – the odds of someone's Chihuahua doing any real damage to your property is basically zero.

The point of allowing pets, of course, is to charge more money, and to that end you should add two things to the lease – a pet deposit and a monthly pet charge. The pet deposit should absorb any of the costs of actual damage done by the animal, which leaves the monthly pet charge as pure profit.

I recommend charging roughly 5% of the rent, translated to a nice round number. If rent is $950, throw in an extra $50 for pets. In terms of the deposit, half a month's rent is usually reasonable, unless rents are very low. If the rent is $2000 a month, $1000 should cover you from damages, especially from small pets. If rent is only $250, it's probably worth charging a full month's rent.

If you have an otherwise good tenant with a big dog you don't really want in your unit, it doesn't hurt to ask them if they're willing to put up a significant deposit and pay a hefty monthly premium. It can be very difficult to find a place that will let you keep a 100 pound dog, so a prospective tenant with a pet of that size may be willing to pay hundreds extra per month and put up thousands as a deposit, especially since people who own dogs of those size tend to be relatively well off. Just remember, it never hurts to ask – your prospect may appreciate that you did instead of just turning them down immediately.

**Service Animals**

One important thing to note is that service animals (as well as emotional support animals in states that have laws allowing those) are exempt from any extra charges or rent. Additionally, it is unlawful to decline a prospective tenant on the basis of their having a service animal. If you have concerns around service animals or are looking at prospective tenants that have them, it's always best to consult an attorney rather than risk a lawsuit for discrimination.

# Fees and Utilities

One of the main recurring costs for any property owner is utilities, including electricity, gas, sewage and garbage. These can add up quickly. Usually sewage, garbage and water are flat fees and thus consistent over time, but electricity and gas are variable costs, which means that they can go way up when the tenant is using more – the most common example of this is watching those bills go up in the winter when the heater comes on.

**Pass Along Your Costs**

The good news is that it's generally permissible to pass these costs along to tenants, though there are some exceptions, so naturally I must caveat that this is not legal advice. I highly recommend this, especially the variable costs.

Besides the obvious benefit of your costs going down and thus your profit going up, there's another less straightforward benefit. When tenants are responsible for paying their gas and electric bills, they will generally be more conscious of the amount of gas and electricity they're using. This means that instead of turning the heater on when it's only mildly chilly, they may put on sweaters. Besides not using gas or electricity, this also reduces wear and tear on your heater and other appliances. This means less frequent repairs, and less maintenance is always better.

This is especially true if you have features in your home that can draw a huge amount of energy if not managed correctly. A hot tub is one – you might only use it once a month, but if you're not paying the bills it's easy to forget to turn it off in between those uses.

Central heating is another – it's always nice to come home to a warm house, and if you're not footing the heating bills then there's no real reason not to keep the heat on all day to that end. For this reason, if you haven't passed the bills along to your tenants then I at least recommend buying a smart thermostat, like the one by Nest. It can be set to heat the house up a few minutes before you arrive home, thus saving a day of heat, and it will learn your schedule over time and automatically turn the heat off when you're away. It's also an attractive and modern feature in the house, which tenants will appreciate.

## Handle Utilities Correctly in Your Listing

While you may want to be as upfront as possible about all the costs your tenant will pay, it's important not to include the price of utilities in the listed rent, especially on sites like Craigslist. That's because virtually no landlords do this, which means that if your unit with $1000 in rent and $100 in utilities is compared to another unit with the same rent and utilities, if you list yours at $1100, the tenant will see $1000 on the other listing and think yours is more expensive, even though it isn't.

If you're less concerned about being upfront with pricing, it can make sense to leave any mention of utilities out of your listing entirely. Prospective tenants will naturally become aware of utilities when they read the lease, but at that point they're unlikely to change their mind about renting your unit.

# Property Management

Hiring professional property managers costs money, so I can understand if you're skeptical that doing so would help you make more money. In many situations, though, your property managers will pay for themselves and then some in the long run.

**Maintenance**

One of the biggest expenses when it comes to owning and renting property is maintenance. Small repairs like fixing a stove or repairing a broken light can add up over time, and big repairs like major electrical work can take out a year's worth of profit or more.

Professional property managers will have experienced all manner of issues with heaters, electrical systems, appliances and every other part of a property. When the tenant calls in to complain about an issue, they'll know how to deal with It as effectively as possible. In some cases, they can completely avoid a trip from a repairman – heater problems may be resolved by simply instructing the tenant on how to re-light the pilot light.

If repairs are needed, especially when it comes to appliances, you'll be left with the question of whether to do the repairs or opt for a full replacement. Repairs are usually cheaper in the short run, but a good property owner will think big picture – doing a $100 repair on a stove every month until it finally breaks isn't a great idea if you could just replace it for $300. Property managers will be much better able to make these tradeoffs than you or I, and that can save you an enormous amount of money.

Beyond maintenance, tenants may also ask for improvements to their units. In rare cases it may be worth making small improvements to keep them happy, but in general you don't want to add anything new at the request of a tenant. Property managers will know how to effectively turn down these requests while maintaining a good relationship with your tenants.

**Rents**

Property managers are experts on your local market, so they'll have an intimate knowledge of whether the current climate is favorable to renters or landlords, as well as what current rents look like. This means that when it's time to rent out your property, they'll know just where to price your unit to ensure you get as much rent as possible without it sitting on the market for too long. Property managers usually charge 7-10% of rents, so if they can help you make 7-10% more than you would otherwise by limiting vacancy and maximizing rents, then clearly they are a good investment.

Of course, the beginning of a lease is not the only time rents come into play – since traditional leases are usually one year long and then convert to month-to-month, every month after the first year is a chance to raise rents. Property managers will have much more expertise in these situations, both because they know what current market rents are, and they will also have the kinds of relationships with your tenants that give them a good idea of what kind of rent increases they will tolerate.

Additionally, if you do raise rents, tenants may want to renegotiate other components of the lease, like converting it back from month-to-month to another year-long lease. They may also request improvements in the property in exchange for the rent increase. Property managers will have a good idea of where to draw the line and when to give tenants what they ask for.

All of this is especially true if you have Section 8 tenants – in these cases, your property managers will have not only relationships with your tenants but also with the Section 8 board. Because of this, they should be able to get a good feel for what size of a rent increase will be approved by the local housing authority. This alone can pay the cost of property management – navigating government bureaucracy is always a headache, so having someone that can not only do it effectively but can also use their skill in doing so to put more money in your pocket is a valuable resource to have in your corner.

**Location and Quality**

Two important things to consider when deciding whether to use property managers are your location relatively to that of the property you're renting and the state of the place. If you live next door and it's a brand new house, property management may not be worth it – things will rarely go wrong for at least a decade after new construction, and if you're close then it's easy for you to keep an eye on the place.

On the other hand, if you inherited your parents' hundred-year-old house on the other side of the country, you should seriously consider property management, as you won't have any idea about the local rents, not to mention laws and regulations. In some places, for example, you have to register as a business with the city if you have rental real estate – if you don't know this is the case, one day you'll wake up to a bill from the city for years of back payments, interest and big penalties. A property manager will save you the headache and the hit to your wallet.

Beyond this, you won't know anything about the contractors you're using and whether they work they're doing is any good. If you need major repairs like a new roof or new electrical, you'll likely want to meet the contractors doing the work. Unfortunately, the price of a cross country flight can wipe out months of profit. Better to hire property managers who have good relationships with reliable contractors and can manage all of the work locally.

# The Roof

It may seem like a small, specific thing, but knowing your roof and being prepared to deal with issues that come up around it can save you an enormous amount of time, energy and money in the long run. Your property will come with a roof (at least I hope so), and it's important to understand both during and after the purchasing process what kind of maintenance it will require and how long you should expect it to last.

Eventually you will have to replace your roof, and while it's easy to just replace it with the same style of roof that was there before, that's not always the right option. Putting a little bit of thought into this can mean saving a lot of money into the short run. If the previous owner was living in the property, he may have opted for something more attractive but less durable, but if you're renting it out you probably care a lot more about cost and durability than looks.

These are a few of the most common types of roofs and their characteristics. The prices listed include only the roof material itself, not labor.

**Asphalt Shingles**
Lifespan: 20-30 years
Asphalt shingles are the most common type of roof in the United States, due to a combination of their appearance, durability and cost. They are relatively inexpensive with a long life span and look good on many types of houses. They look like dark, overlapping squares or rectangles with a rough texture.
There are multiple grades of asphalt shingles, and higher quality ones may last 40-50 years. When you have your roof installed, it should come with a warranty - if you're

paying more for asphalt shingles, they should come with a longer warranty.
Price: $1.20-2.00/sq. ft.

**Tile**

Lifespan: 25-35 years
There are a number of different styles of tile, one of the most common being the traditional red spanish tile. The price of the tiles varies by style, but they are generally on the expensive side of roof styles. The tiles themselves can actually have an extremely long life if property maintained, but the underlying roof support may need to be repaired after 25 years - possibly shorter in very hot regions.
Price: $2.00-$4.20/sq. ft.

**Metal**

Lifespan: 60-70 years
Metal is notable both for its durability and price. It is often a popular choice in place with extreme weather, due to its ability to withstand major weather events. With other styles of roof, storms can cause damage and then allow water to get into the underlying wood, leading to rotting that can cost a significant amount to repair. There are several types of metal roofs, including metal shingles and large metal panels.
Price: $4.00-10.00/sq. ft.

**Cedar Shake**

Lifespan: 30-40 years
Cedar shake consists of wood shingles that are often considered to be more attractive than asphalt shingles. They are relatively durable, but are especially well suited for sunny areas, since they do not break down from UV light. The term "cedar shake" is not always used literally - there are many different types of wood used for shingles.

Cost: $6.00-9.00/sq. ft.

Before you buy, ask the seller how long the existing roof has been on the property – he may not know, but if he can at least tell you that he's never replaced it, you can check public records to find out the previous sale date of the house. That way, you know the minimum amount of time the roof has been there. If it's getting near the end of its life (or if you're not sure how long, but it's at least halfway there), you should send a roof inspector onto it to tell you whether there are any current issues and to give you an estimate of how much longer he expects it to last.

Once you own the property, take note of how frequently roof issues are cropping up. One leak isn't necessary a huge problem, but if they're springing up fairly regularly, eventually it'll make sense to have someone inspect the roof and tell you if it needs replacing. It sounds costly, but constantly having to patch holes is expensive too. Much worse is having part of the roof collapse, especially during bad weather, and having to deal with potential damage to your tenants' property or injuries to your tenants themselves.

# Extra Tips

## Incremental Rent Raises

As mentioned, you can generally raise rents once a year. In my experience as a renter, landlords often wait two to three years before raising the rent, and then they do so by a significant amount. Instead, it's much better to raise the rent by small amounts each year. Consider your renter's perspective – if they decide not to accept the rent raise, they have to go through the hassle of hunting for a new place, not to mention the pain and cost of moving.

A $50 per month raise equates to $600 per year, which is usually less than the cost of hiring movers (not to mention dealing with the pain of packing and apartment hunting) – given that, it rarely makes sense to move out of a property for a rent increase of that amount. On the other hand, waiting a few years and raising it $200 makes that math a bit more favorable to moving.

Bear in mind that if you're in an area that has a very hot real estate market with rapidly increasing rents, big increases may make sense. If the market rent for your unit is $300 higher than it was a year ago when you first rented it to your tenants, an increase of $200 probably makes sense. In that case, you either get a significant increase in rent and retain the continuity of keeping your existing tenants (which saves you the cost of vacancy), or they choose to move out and you get an even larger rent increase.

## Month to Month Rentals

There are many situations in which a prospective tenant might not want to sign a year-long lease, be it a temporary job placement, anticipation of moving in a few months to be near family or something else. Many landlords prefer not to rent to these tenants because they ensure that the property will be vacant and need all the cleaning and preparation for re-renting it that requires.

Because there are few month-to-month rentals, though, those landlords that are willing to provide them have a significant amount of leverage when it comes to pricing. A $1000/month rental might be rentable at $1500 or more on a month-to-month lease. If you're really concerned that the extra money won't cover the cost of vacancy, you can offer a sliding schedule for tenants who wish to sign a lease shorter than a year. For example:

- 12 month lease - $1000
- 11 month lease - $1075
- 10 month lease - $1150
- 9 month lease - $1225
- 8 month lease - $1300
- 7 month lease - $1375
- 6 month lease - $1450
- 5 month lease - $1525
- 4 month lease - $1600
- 3 month lease - $1675
- 2 month lease - $1750
- Month-to-month lease - $1825

By offering this kind of flexibility, you will draw in a bigger crowd of potential renters. If you strongly prefer an annual lease, you can always prioritize tenants who will stay for a year. If you only end up with one interested prospect who wants to sign a six month lease, though, that's certainly better than having no one because you didn't offer the shorter-term options.

## Open Houses

Many agents simply have people call them to schedule showings, but open houses are frequently a better way of showing the property to prospects. First of all, they're efficient for you – lots of people at once instead of repeated showings to individuals. Second, if you're in a hot rental market, it creates a sense of urgency for renters when they see a significant number of other people who are also interested in the unit.

I was looking for an apartment in San Francisco in 2010, and I quickly found that I had to be ready with an application, a copy of my credit report and a check for the deposit in hand. If you weren't prepared with these things, someone would have them and would offer their application on the spot. All else being equal, landlords would usually take the first applicant, so speed was of the essence. Sometimes this led later applicants to offer even more money than the listed rent. This is one of the most extreme examples of this effect, but it's nonetheless a good illustration of how you can derive value from creating the sense of competition and thus inspiring a sense of urgency in your prospective renters.

## Record Keeping

It's tough to know how much money you're making if you don't have records. A little money goes in for repairs, some rent money comes out, the mortgage gets paid, property taxes come up and suddenly it's tough to know if you've turned a profit over the last year.

To make sure you're on top of things, you should be recording every dollar that goes in or comes out of the property. First, ensure you're tracking your recurring costs on a monthly basis – things like gardeners, utilities and mortgage payments. These will give you a baseline of how much of the rent you receive each month goes to your costs. Beyond that, keep track of costs that are both variable and annually recurring on a yearly basis.

Annual recurring costs are things like taxes, accountants' tax prep fees and insurance. Variable costs are things like maintenance and legal costs for things like evictions. Even if your property's net income looks good on a monthly basis, annual costs can take a big chunk out of your total profit, and variable costs (especially something as costly as an eviction) can turn an otherwise profitable property into a money pit.

Keeping detailed records will help you understand if there are monthly costs you should work to reduce (perhaps the gardener can come less frequently or you can switch to smaller trash bins). Keeping control of these will help maximize the money that flows in regularly. Variable costs can tell you when it's time to make significant investments – if you're constantly repairing a leaky roof, it may be time to spend the upfront money to replace it.

These are just a few examples, but ultimately understanding your costs will enable you to understand your property, and that's the best way to ensure that you successfully turn a profit in the long run.

### Tenant Referrals

It's always a shame when a high quality tenant has to move out, but that doesn't mean you're completely out of luck. People often associate with other people similar to themselves, so your well-employed and responsible tenant probably knows other well-employed, responsible people. These can be great sources of leads. At the very least, let your tenants know that you'll be looking for someone new and you'd be happy to give priority to their friends. In a hot rental market, this can be quite a perk – your tenant's friends have likely been to the apartment, and if they like it then the chance to get a good apartment without competition will be enticing. People will also generally be more comfortable renting a place that a friend has lived in – you can only learn so much about a property in a twenty minute tour, but if you have a friend who's lived there for years then you can be sure there won't be any surprises after you move in.

If you want, you can take this a step further and offer referral bonuses for tenants – if they can get a tenant who will move in a within a week of the end of their lease, you can give them $100 or more.

**Cosmetic Improvements**

You can spend a lot of money on incredibly important aspects of your property like updating your electrical systems and replacing the roof, but these aren't things tenants will notice. For a fraction of the cost of major work, you can make minor improvements that will really improve the rentability of your property. Consider the fact that most prospective tenants will spend 15-20 minutes there before making a decision about whether to rent. Given that, focus on small but noticeable things:

- Add minor landscaping, like small shrubs or flower pots

- Replace cheap blinds with updated shutters
- Paint/refinish cabinets
- Change hardware – drawer pulls and door handles can make a big difference

These types of updates can provide an enormous amount of bang for your buck. They cost very little but are very noticeable during a short walkthrough. This means not only that your property will be more attractive and thus more liable to be rented quickly, but also that you may be able to charge more for it.

The other advantage to these types of repairs are that aren't costly to replace. If you spend a lot of money upgrading your appliances to beautiful new stainless steel ones with endless lists of features, you'll not only spend a lot up front, but you'll also be on the hook for any repairs to those appliances when they inevitably break. Door handles rarely break, and when they do they're cheap to replace.

## Conclusion

We've reached the end of our time together (unless you want to read this again, which I can't argue with), and I hope you've taken some useful information away from this book. I've only just scratched the surface of the real estate investing world – if this has piqued your interest, there are lots more resources that will help you dive even deeper. I can't recommend enough, though, that you go out and start talking to some real estate agents. Even if you're not ready to buy yet, most agents will be more than happy to have coffee with you and tell you more about real estate in your area.

If you enjoyed this book, please rate it on Amazon! Also, check out my other book on how to find and hire the best property manager for your real estate – Finding Your Property Manager.

Good luck!

Made in the USA
Monee, IL
06 October 2020